DESTINATION
CALIFORNIA
NATIONAL PARKS

A Joshua tree in the national monument of the same name.

DESTINATION
CALIFORNIA
NATIONAL PARKS

Photographs: Gerhard P. Müller
Text: Tim McKay
Michael Wolf

WINDSOR BOOKS
INTERNATIONAL

Fern Canyon with Patrick Creek in the far north of California, with the magnificent growth of ferns that gave it its name.

CONTENTS

The famous California Highway 1 runs along the steep coast between Monterey and Morro Bay.

CREATION OF THE CALIFORNIA WILDERNESS

For over four hundred and fifty years, writers have been committing their impressions of California to paper, from Garcia Ordonez de Montalvo, whose whimsical 1520 novel *Las Sergas de Esplandian* gave California its name, to modern authors suggesting influences from outer space. Even a hundred years ago people still had some very strange ideas about California's landscape and natural wonders. The land seemed so far away and the information trickling out was incomplete and often unreliable. Distorted images of the state still have not entirely disappeared: just as in a marionette theatre, the real actors pulling the strings are hidden behind the scenes of the "Golden State".

A "modern" primeval forest established itself in California at least 50 million years before man appeared. It is assumed that man first settled here only 30,000 years ago – a very short time span when compared with the 4,000 to 6,000 million years numbered by the earth itself!

The first immigrants, erroneously named "Indians" by their European discoverers, probably came to California through the dry southwestern regions, perhaps passing through the Colorado Valley. Their oldest known settlements were located in the south; the most recent, dating back some 500 to 2,000 years, seem to have been in the northern coastal area. These peoples, and the native Americans who followed, settled and developed their own way of life adapted to the area. Successive waves of immigration and developmental trends finally resulted in the establishment of sixty main Indian tribes with names such as the Tolowa, Modoc, Washo and Miwok. Their lifestyles were as sharply differentiated as were the regions where they lived.

At the time of the first recorded visit of Europeans to California in 1542, the Indian population numbered approximately 310,000. It was not however until 1769, with the founding of the Catholic mission stations, that white people began to settle in California. Eighty years later, the so-called "Forty-Niners" arrived, a wave of immigrants interested in making a quick fortune during the gold rush. For the Indians, this marked the end of their peaceful seclusion, a life in harmony with nature. Most fell victim to the European attempts at "civilization": they either died of infections never previously encountered or were murdered in cold blood. As a result, by 1870 California had a population of 560,000 white people and less than 50,000 Indians.

When we admire California's spectacular scenery we should always remember these people. Their spirit surely lives on in the magnificent panoramas: their roots went deep into the land providing them with sustenance.

The early white settlers were a restless people, out to make money and to buy happiness, possessions or at the very least, a ticket to return home. Some of them, however, introduced a new philosophy of life based on the view that mankind was a part of nature. The poets Ralph Waldo Emerson, George Perkins Marsh and Henry David Thoreau were responsible for spreading this idea to a wider population. In their writings, metaphysical and practical relationships are established between man and his environment. While Thoreau theorized in 1851 that the world is preserved through its wilderness areas, Marsh felt that man had long since forgotten that the earth was only given him so that he could enjoy its benefits, not to exhaust them and certainly not to waste them.

These were the ideas which brought John Muir to California in 1868. He devoted the subsequent decades of his life to the study of these regions, and through his work introduced a new awareness of nature.

Water – The Beginning and The End

The air masses moving east from the Pacific Ocean are forced to rise over the steep mountains. As they cool,

El Capitan is the most famous climbing face in the United States, 2,307 metres (7,569 feet) high. This almost vertical wall of granite is a dominant feature of Yosemite National Park in the Sierra Nevadas.

the water vapour condenses and falls on the land as rain, though not evenly distributed. The steep mountains and weather patterns of California have produced climatic islands where remnants of the old coniferous forests of the north and the tropical primeval forests of the south can still be found. According to the distribution of moisture, the redwoods grow in the northwestern corner of California and the hot, dry south is a cactus garden.

The water cut fissures in the mountains that were formed and in places folded over the course of millions of years, but it also created fertile plains. Today California lies between the subtropical high pressure area of the Hawaiian Islands and a northern depression, with cold wet winds bringing the California Current from the Gulf of Alaska. In the winter the Hawaiian high shifts to the south so that the depression advances further towards California; in the summer it moves further north, producing the blue sky for which California is famous.

For many people the majesty of California's mountains is associated with the extraordinary variety of the region's plants. Henry James visited California in 1905 and could find very little cultural or intellectual life but felt the brilliantly-coloured wild flowers were worthy of a purer planet than our earth.

John Muir, who was to become the pioneer of the conservation movement, had had a similar vision almost forty years prior to James. With the onset of blindness, he had sought the beauty of God in nature. When in April 1868 he stood on Pacheco Pass in the Coast Ranges, a few days after first setting foot on California soil in April 1868, he was overwhelmed by the sea of flowers which spread over the Central Valley, reaching to the green foothills and beyond to the snow-covered Sierra Mountains.

Muir equated the scene to a lake of sunshine, with the blue of the sky softly blending into the yellow of the valley like the colours of a rainbow. Further, the colours formed for him a great bank of inexpressibly fine light.

The view from Pacheco Pass is quite different today, with its panorama of tomato, sweet potato, olive and cotton fields in addition to herds of grazing cattle. The air is no longer so pure while the view of the shining snow-covered mountains is now dimmed by haze.

In spite of the environmental consciousness that is now gaining ground, we should also be grateful for the halfway-sensible nature conservation schemes. The untouched areas which exist today result from past debates concerning individual areas, not from planned measures aimed at the preservation of the whole ecosystem. Various nature preserves have been created and are administered through a wide spectrum of different private, local, state and federal programmes. This collection of laws, parks, refuges, national forests, wilderness areas and wild rivers is as a whole quite impressive, but it has been put together in a rather random fashion, not representing a systematic plan.

After more than eighty years of tireless effort and the cooperation of several institutions, it was finally possible in 1968 to place under protection a pieced-together area containing the old coastal redwoods. These giant trees were also found in Alaska, Greenland, England, China and Norway during the Tertiary Period. Today the only place where they still thrive is along the coast of northern California, where over eighty hectares (198 acres) of redwood forest, along 650 kilometres (405 miles) of coastline, are under protection. In many of the reserves the trees were once felled.

Most of the over 100 metre (325 foot) high trees (they are some of the highest in the world), with an approximate age of 2,000 years, are found in the Humboldt and Del-Norte Districts. Redwood National Park (recently declared a World Heritage Park by UNESCO) occupies 42,000 hectares (103,782 acres) of land, but ancient trees are found on only 16,000 hectares (39,536 acres). Extensive areas of the park were severely damaged when the land was still privately owned. The federal statute encorporating the area into national parks also made thirty-three million dollars available for attempts at conserving the karstic slopes of Redwood Bay. In spite of all these efforts, there are no longer any large stands consisting solely of old trees.

Civilized man's weakness for things of great size made the redwood a popular and protected tree, but further to the east of the Coast Ranges, in the mountainous Klamath-Siskiyou Region, there are coniferous forests which are no less unique both from the point of view of their geographical significance and their limited biotope. They, too, are worthy of protection.

Over twenty different types of conifer flourish in these forests, some of the richest habitats in the world. The Douglas pine reaches heights of up to 100 metres (325 feet) and is very popular with the lumberjacks, while the rare *picea breweriana* grows just below the tree line. No moves have been made to preserve these forests, some of the most important relics of the primeval forest in existence, which have scarcely changed in composition for 100 million years, though public awareness is beginning to raise concerns.

Bridalveil Falls plunge 189 metres (614 feet) into the Yosemite Valley, at the centre of the national park of the same name.

The wind for hang-gliding from Glacier Point in Yosemite Park is ideal first thing in the morning. Early risers are rewarded by an unforgettable flight in magnificent surroundings.

The Volcanic Landscapes
of the Northeast

The few rivers that flow through the northeastern part of California have all been harnessed for the use of man. The upper reaches of the Sacramento, McCloud and Pitt Rivers all feed into Lake Shasta, a man-made lake which is a key element in the Central Valley Project.

In this large area, encompassing a total of 3.6 million hectares (8.9 million acres), there are a number of impressive peaks, the highest being Mount Shasta (4,300 metres/13,975 feet), possibly an extinct volcano. Its summit is covered with snow all year round.

Mount Shasta is typical of the peaks in the volcanic Cascade Range extending far to the north through the states of Oregon and Washington (where Mount St Helens erupted on 27 March 1980 and in March 1982) and to the south as far as Mount Lassen. This particular volcano erupted on a number of spectacular occasions between 1914 and 1917.

The countryside around Mount Lassen is predominantly characterized by formations of volcanic origin. It was primarily on account of these features that Lassen Volcanic National Park (43,000 hectares or 106,253 acres) and Lava Beds National Monument (19,000 hectares or 46,949 acres) came into being.

To the north and east of the Cascade Range, a large part of the Modoc Region is taken up by a wide plateau of basalt rising from 300 metres (975 feet) in the southwest to 3,000 metres (9,750 feet) in the east, resulting from volcanic intrusion.

This plateau opens out towards the west and drains both into the Klamath and Pitt Rivers (a tributary of the Sacramento) and thus into the main federal and state irrigation canals. Most of the water flows into these channels during the spring thaw. During the winters, when temperatures often fall below −30° Centigrade (−22° Fahrenheit), much of the precipitation falls as snow, on an average of around 25 to 30 centimetres (10–12 inches) annually. On the other hand, the summers in this part of California are hot and dry.

Weather conditions have a considerable influence on the vegetation. The northeast part of California is predominantly prairie land, with inland sage brush, various types of artemisia and cercocarpus and rabbit

Glacier Point, well worth the long round-about road to the top, is a plateau 2,200 metres (7,214 feet) above sea level, with a breath-taking view of the Yosemite Valley and Half Dome.

brush the most common forms of vegetation. And in the spring the barren land is suddenly transformed into a luminous carpet of wildflowers, with the otherwise rare sand lily quite prominent. Various types of conifer and juniper grow primarily at higher altitudes, while the aspen follows the waterways of the area.

The vegetation in turn has an influence on the wildlife, of which there are some interesting species. The pronghorn antelope was once common in California but has been reduced in the northeast to the single herd of around 6,000 animals. Scientists assume that the pronghorn antelope is the sole surviving member of a family of animals, the *antilocapridae*, native only to North America; presumably, twelve million years ago, there were many different varieties on this continent. A further inhabitant of the artemisia prairie is the ubiquitous coyote found roaming at the base of Mount Shasta and living on the numerous jack rabbits and other small rodents in abundant supply on the plateau. There remains a small population of desert bighorn sheep: on a visit at the end of the last century, John Muir described the stony lava fields and hills as "swarming" with these animals. They have now become almost extinct through contact with the illnesses and parasites carried by domestic sheep. Conservationists have met with little success in their attempts to reintroduce the bighorn into the region.

Large mule deer, the delight of hunters, live in the Warner Range, an area protected as part of the wilderness system. The uniqueness of the region was acknowledged in 1931 when it was separated off as a Primitive Area within the 6,600 square kilometre (2,547 square mile) Modoc National Forest. The South Warner Wilderness Area is used for a variety of purposes but no motorized devices are allowed within its boundaries. On the western side the mountains rise gently to summits between 2,700 and 3,000 metres high (8,775 to 9,750 feet) while on the eastern side they steeply drop down to the deserts and salt lakes of Nevada. During the spring and summer the slopes are covered with a rich variety of flora, in particular the sunflower *wyethia angustifolia* common to this area. Most of the animal species of this region find refuge in the protected area. As well as the shepherds living in the South Warner Wilderness, among them a striking number of Basques, the refuge also attracts many scientists, students, photographers, hunters and fishermen.

The Sierras – The "Mountains of Light"

The Sierra Mountains, one of the most impressive chains of the Rockies, form the western border of the prairie-like Great Basin covering the whole of Nevada and parts of Utah. The range also plays a key role in the state irrigation system. An average of 500 to 1,800 centimetres (200 to 700 inches) of snow falls annually on the northern summits. The melted snow feeds the fourteen most important river systems flowing west into the Central Valley: the Sacramento, Feather, Yuba, American, Consumnes, Mokelumne, Calaveras, Stanislaus, Tuolumne, Merced, San Joaquin, King's, Kaweah and Kern Rivers. These systems have all been dammed to provide the settlements and towns sited along them with water and energy.

The Sierra Nevadas consists primarily of a uniform granite core formed deep in the earth beneath an old chain of volcanoes. During the 300 million years following its formation, the volcanoes were gradually eroded away. Like the lower Warner Mountains in the northeast, the Sierra range consists of folded mountains. The more recent and massive Sierra-Batholiths fall steeply both to the east and west; the eastern cliffs are the more precipitous. This wall of bare granite, between 80 and 95 kilometres (50–60 miles) wide, extends for 640 kilometres (400 miles) along the Central Valley. In the northern part of the Sierras, the peaks are around 2,000 metres (6,500 feet) high, while in the southern part, from Lake Tahoe to Sequoia National Park, more than five hundred are over 3,500 metres (13,000 feet). The highest point in the Sierra Nevadas, and for that matter in the lower continental United States, is Mount Whitney, with a height of 4,418 metres (14,358 feet); it is situated near at the southern tip of the chain at a distance of 135 kilometres (80 miles) from the lowest point in North America, found in Death Valley. At the junction of the southern foothills and the Transverse Ranges running from east to west, the Tehachapi Mountains, closes off the Central Valley.

The efforts of John Muir, his contemporaries and successors has been highly fruitful in the Sierras, where an 11,000 square kilometre (4,247 square mile) zone of national parks and nature reserves has been created; it is an area of overwhelming beauty and tranquility. The nine national forests of the Sierras include several nature reserves, one of which is named for John Muir. Most of them are situated at heights of over 2,100 metres (6,825 feet), where even on horseback progress is difficult and would-be explorers are forced to proceed on foot.

The watersheds of the Sierra Mountains are or were covered, to heights of 2,100 metres (6,825 feet), by ancient forests containing various types of utilizable timber. Here, also where the massive pitch pine and sugar pine, which grow to heights of over 60 metres (195 feet), were once felled. The lumber industry is the most important in the national forests, mainly in this transitional zone extending down to an altitude of 400 metres (1,300 feet). In addition to the giant pines, the deciduous oak *Quercus kelloggii* and the evergreen strawberry tree, with its characteristic large leaves and growing mainly on dry slopes, are also found here. Above the transitional zone are the semi-Arctic to Arctic climatic regions where the vegetation is exposed to wind, ice and snow. Among the trees growing here are the rare species of the bearded pine and the related *Pinus aristata*, the oldest known organism in existence. Other types of conifer to be found in these high regions are the hemlock and *Abies concolor*, a species of fir. Under ideal conditions, they can grow to heights of up to 55 metres (178 feet), but in exposed places, exist in stunted forms less than one metre (3 feet) tall.

On the western edge of the southern Sierras, at heights of 800 to 2,700 metres (2,600 to 8,775 feet), seventy-five small groves, with a total area of 1,400 hectares (3,459.4 acres), contain the largest living organisms in the world. Although not as tall, the sequoia is five times more massive than the redwood of the north coast belonging to the same family. It was not until 1949 that a third type was discovered, the *metasequoia glyptostroboides*; it had previously only been found in China in fossil form. The California sequoias are all protected and are primarily concentrated in Yosemite, Sequoia and King's Canyon National Parks, all established in 1890.

The parks are also important for the fauna of the Sierra Mountains. Many of the animals which live here are also native to the Klamath-Siskiyou Region and the volcanic countryside of the northeast. The largest herbivore is the mule deer. In the spring and summer it grazes in the lush meadows while in the autumn and winter survives by eating the branches and leaves of the quaking aspen, dogwood, serviceberry and bilberry, various types of willow and snowberry. Although now almost extinct, the puma is still its main enemy. The puma once ranged over an area larger than any other mammal in the western hemisphere, a habitat reaching from British Columbia in Canada to Patagonia in South America. The largest of the feline family, to which the domestic cat also belongs, the puma can reach a length of 2.80 metres (9 feet) from its nose to the tip of its tail with a

Half Dome, the symbol of Yosemite National Park, is an enormous granite dome-shaped rock spectacularly cut in half by glacial erosion during the last ice age. It is immortalized in the impressive photographs of the great American nature photographer, Ansel Adams.

The colours of the Painted Dunes in Lassen Volcanic National Park are due to the presence of various metal oxides.

weight of up to 100 kilograms (220 pounds). In order to survive it requires 100 square kilometres (38.61 square miles) of territory. The puma has been protected in California for years, ever since its numbers started to decline. Nevertheless, cattle breeders repeatedly apply for permission to shoot them, saying they attack not only the mule deer but also their herds. The puma, coyote and fox also hunt other wild animals including the beaver, squirrel, kangaroo rat, vole, chipmunk, rabbit, hare and pika, those small rodents living in the highest alpine zones.

Other particularly rare animals to be found in the Sierras are the large tawny owl, which normally lives on the Canadian prairies, a brightly-coloured alpine variant of the rainbow trout and the bighorn sheep, which continues to inhabit a narrow strip of the southeastern ranges. The parks also host a thriving population of black bears. Having been fed by the tourists they can now live on the large quantities of rubbish left lying around. They have proliferated to such an extent that now even this source of nutrition is not enough for their needs.

It would probably never have occurred to John Muir and the other pioneers of Sierra National Park that these protected areas might one day become the last refuges for several animals. And they could never have foreseen that Yosemite National Park would be visited annually by almost three million people. The people, fleeing from a modern urban existence and themselves seeking a sense of recuperation, have become a problem, polluting the air of the park with their cars and trampling all over the fields of flowers in the alpine meadows.

Yosemite National Park is famous for its smooth bare walls of rock more than 1,000 metres (3,250 feet) high, and the six waterfalls that plunge over them into the valley, including the 739 metre high (2,425 feet) Yosemite Falls to the 180 metre high (785 feet) Nevada Falls. The polished rock walls are the result of the last great ice age some 11,000 years ago and their non-uniform geological substratum. And if these cliffs are not spectacular enough, the alpenglow on summer evenings is something never to be forgotten: cliffs, peaks and sky seem to be on fire. It was for this reason that Muir called the Sierra range the "the mountains of light", a description that still inspires photographers from all over the world to try and capture this miracle on film.

In the language of the Washo Indians, who lived in the area for centuries before the advent of the railways, casinos and motorways, "tahoe" means "big water". The rocks and rivers which flowed into the big lake were given names by the Washo Indians due to their important roles played in the ancient Indian creation myths. Lake Tahoe's considerable depth (over 500 metres or 625 feet) gives the crystal-clear water its sapphire-blue colour.

The combination of such scenery and a legal situation that is not very clearly defined (the responsibility for the area is shared by the Tahoe National Forest, the states of California and Nevada, and the communities of Tahoe City, South Lake Tahoe and Stateline) has resulted in the unrestricted growth which has proved impossible to contain. On the positive side, however, Lake Tahoe has a highly effective sewage system, whereby all the waste water in the whole catchment area of the lake is collected in pipes, and, following a thorough purification, is pumped out of the ground into a reservoir in Nevada. In this way a build-up of those products conducive to the growth of algae is prevented.

One of the main unsolved developmental problems in the basin is the burgeoning construction of holiday homes. The resulting destruction of the ground in turn leads to an increased use of the fertilizers eventually finding their way into the lake. A further problem is posed by the firms competing with one another to put up skyscrapers and casinos in Nevada, where gambling is legal.

Southern California

The Transverse Ranges mark the boundary between Northern and Southern California. The southern part of the state consists of two main regions: the desert, encompassing almost 113,000 square kilometres (43,629 square miles), and the southwest, an area of around 43,000 square kilometres (16,602 square miles) or approximately the size of Switzerland. Together these two regions form thirty-eight percent of the total area of the state, but contain fifty-eight percent of California's population. Thirteen million people live south of the Tehachapi and Transverse Ranges, most of whom are concentrated along the coastal areas of Los Angeles and San Diego; there are also one or two towns in the desert. The average annual rainfall varies from just over 40 centimetres (15.75 inches) in the northwest desert region and White Mountains, to less than seven centimetres (2.75 inches) in Imperial Valley on the Mexican border. The quantity of water evaporating into the atmosphere is usually higher than that falling as rain.

Death Valley National Monument, Joshua Tree National Monument and Anza-Borrego Desert State Park are the three main nature reserves in the

Lassen Volcanic National Park is aptly named: here the earth is still very active, as the hot springs, bubbling mud and steaming lakes amply demonstrate.

Bumpass Hell, an inferno created by sulphur deposits, is undeniable evidence of continuing volcanic activity beneath the earth's surface. A sensitive nose is a disadvantage here.

California desert region. There are projects for further reserves and the appropriate legal framework is currently being prepared. One of the most frustrating of all environmental enterprises, however, has been the attempt to save Mono Lake.

Mono Lake, the last of numerous glacial lakes of the Pleistocene Period, is located at the eastern edge of the Sierra Nevadas. It is 1,950 metres (6,337 feet) above sea level and has an area of approximately 100 square kilometres (38.61 square miles). During the ice ages, it was fed by glacial meltwater from the Sierras and thus contained fresh water. However, our modern hot dry climate has caused so much evaporation that the lake water is now three times saltier and six times more alkaline than sea water. Fish can no longer survive in this environment but there are various water plants, brine shrimp, brine flies and more than one hundred species of birds which either breed in the area or pass through it during migration. The California gull, Wilson's phalarope and a type of diver are the most frequent birds breeding at Mono Lake. The Mono Paiute, an Indian tribe who once lived on the lake's shore, gathered the larvae of water insects, which in dried form provided them with a rich source of protein.

In 1941 the municipal energy and water authorities of Los Angeles began to tap four of the five inlets of Mono Lake. As a result, the level of the lake has dropped dramatically. More than 120 thousand million litres (26.40 thousand million gallons) are now annually pumped out of the Mono Basin into Owen's Valley; from here the water flows downhill toward Los Angeles.

As these large quantities of water continue to be removed, the lake will become increasingly salty and alkaline until the point is reached when the small living creatures in it will die and the birds will, thus, also disappear. The protection of birds is no longer the exclusive preserve of older ladies. In North America it is now the most popular way of becoming involved with nature, whether as an "amateur bird protector" or a keen birdwatcher prepared to travel hundreds of miles in order to see a rare specimen. The desert oases are not only the destination of the migrating birds, but also their admirers.

This is particularly applicable to Death Valley National Monument, declared a protected area in 1935. Death Valley occupies an area of 7,700 square kilometres (2,793 square miles) and rises from a depression of 86 metres (279 feet) below sea level to

These basalt pillars in Lassen Volcanic National Park are also of volcanic origin: here the lava formed crystalline columns as it solidified.

Telescope Peak, with a height of 3,368 metres (10,746 feet).

It was not long after the discovery of Death Valley in 1849 that prospectors began to exploit its minerals. While they searched in vain for gold and silver, the discovery of borates in the 1880s and again between 1914 and 1927 transformed the valley into a scene of hectic activity. The region's extremely high temperatures are ideal for the formation of mineral salts.

In damper climatic periods this area was flooded, but today the valley floor receives less than five centimetres (two inches) of precipitation every year; the air temperature can reach 56 degrees Centigrade (132 degrees Fahrenheit).

In spite of the heat a surprising number of different animals evolved in this region. Today Death Valley is home to 307 species of bird, 53 mammals, 36 reptiles, 3 amphibians and even 6 types of fish, of which 5 are rare species of carp. The rarest of them evolved from an ancestor in the oldest lakes of the area: it is the desert pupfish inhabiting a source cave without a surface outlet.

The Panamint Mountains on the west side of the valley are among the oldest formations in California.

They date from the Pre-Cambrian Period and are probably around 1.8 thousand million years old. The mountains are a further refuge for the remaining population of bighorn sheep, threatened with extinction throughout the state. The wild burros introduced by miners in the 1880s multiplied alarmingly in the barren grazing lands at the expense of the wild sheep; they are considered a serious problem to the conservationists now trying to find a way of enabling the bighorn sheep to survive without also endangering the burros.

Death Valley is also the home of a very small population of deer, the occasional puma and the cunning coyote, but above all of bats and certain small rodents. As an example of the highly developed ability of the animals here to adapt to their environment, the kangaroo rat meets its need for liquid solely through the plants it eats.

Seven separate plant communities, determined by the different temperature and humidity conditions, are to be found in Death Valley and also in the Mojave and Colorado Deserts.

The desert flowers are no less beautiful than those of the mountain meadows and northern coastal valleys of California. The desert blooms for a very short time when there has been a sufficient quantity of rain. Such an event, frequently occurring in the spring and on mild, sunny winter days, draw millions of people every year from the towns of southwestern California. This pleasant side of the desert was overlooked for a long time, and it was not until the beginning of this century that writers began to praise its virtues.

Mary Austin's book, *Land of Little Rain* published in 1903, describes the austere beauty of the dry areas and the Indian inhabitants. She and her contemporaries opened the eyes of the Californians to the desert, just as John Muir had opened their eyes to the Sierras.

Joshua Tree National Monument is a 213,000 hectare (526,323 acre) area of desert and mountain forest with an abundance of Joshua trees growing up to nine metres (29 feet) tall, and Mojave yuccas (up to four metres or 13 feet high). These unusual plants have clusters of hard, sword-like leaves up to one metre (three feet) long, with white blossoms resembling lilies on stalks one to two metres (three to six feet) long. The reserve extends over a large area of the Little San Bernardino Mountains separating the Mojave Desert from the lower-lying Colorado Desert in the south.

The third largest desert park in California is the state-administered Anza-Borrego State Desert Park, separated from the Joshua Tree National Monument by the Coachella and Imperial Valleys, both having a remarkable morphology resulting from the San Andreas Fault.

From the Peninsular Mountains of Anza-Borrego, Salton Sea is visible to the east and on a clear day, San Diego appears to the west. In this region another spectacular desert plant community is to be found: the fan palm is a relict of the wetter climatic periods thousands of years ago.

In the spring the bushes resound with the songs of a wide variety of birds. The voice of the cactus-dweller is heard from amidst thorny branches while hummingbirds collect nectar from the blossoms of an ocotillo patch. The mountains slopes are sown with brilliant yellow rayana grass and the desert plain is dotted with the royal-blue blossoms of the smoke tree. For a moment time seems to stand still and the overcrowded industrial centres to the west cease to exist.

THE TAMING OF THE WILDERNESS
Reflections and Studies of the California National Parks

The spectacular beauty of California's canyons, waterfalls, forests and mountains helped to inspire the American national park system. The intention of the government was to preserve the wilderness, yet allow the public an opportunity to experience and explore the natural wonders. The excerpts provided here describe the scenic beauty of the California wilderness, its strange and mysterious powers, including a comment on the threat posed by modern-day commercial and tourist interests.

The Range of Light

When I set out on the long excursion that finally led to California, I wandered, afoot and alone, from Indiana to the Gulf of Mexico, with a plant-press on my back, holding a generally southward course, like the birds when they are going from summer to winter. From the west coast of Florida I crossed the Gulf to Cuba, enjoyed the rich tropical flora there for a few months, intending to go thence to the north end of South America, make my way through the woods to the head waters of the Amazon, and float down that grand river to the ocean. But I was unable to find a ship bound for South America – fortunately, perhaps, for I had incredibly little money for so long a trip and had not yet fully recovered from a fever caught in the Florida swamps. Therefore I decided to visit California for a year or two to see its wonderful flora and the famous Yosemite Valley. All the world was before me and every day was a holiday, so it did not seem important to which one of the world's wildernesses I first should wander.

Arriving by the Panama steamer, I stopped one day in San Francisco and then inquired for the nearest

Lassen Peak on the far shore of Helen Lake, where the water has a high mineral content. The volcano, which last erupted in 1914, looks harmless enough today, but appearances can be deceptive: it is by no means classified as extinct.

Emerald Bay, Lake Tahoe, is aptly named: Mark Twain referred to the lake as a noble sheet of blue water.

way out of town. "But where do you want to go?" asked the man to whom I had applied for this important information. "To any place that is wild," I said. This reply startled him. He seemed to fear I might be crazy, and therefore the sooner I was out of the town the better, so he directed me to the Oakland ferry.

So on the 1st of April, 1868, I set out afoot for Yosemite. It was the bloom-time of the year over the lowlands and coast ranges; the landscapes of the Santa Clara Valley were fairly drenched with sunshine, all the air was quivering with the songs of the meadowlarks and the hills were so covered with flowers that they seemed to be painted. Slow, indeed, was my progress through these glorious gardens, the first of the California flora I had seen. Cattle and cultivation were making few scars as yet, and I wandered enchanted in long, wavering curves, knowing by my pocket map that Yosemite Valley lay to the east and that I should surely find it. . . .

Looking eastward from the summit of the Pacheco Pass one shining morning, a landscape was displayed that after all my wanderings still appears as the most beautiful I have ever beheld. At my feet lay the Great Central Valley of California, level and flowery, like a lake of pure sunshine, forty or fifty miles wide, five hundred miles long, one rich furred garden of yellow compositae.

And from the eastern boundary of this vast golden flower bed rose the mighty Sierra, miles in height, and so gloriously colored and so radiant, it seemed not clothed with light, but wholly composed of it, like the wall of some celestial city. Along the top and extending a good way down, was a rich pearl-gray belt of snow; below it a belt of blue and dark purple, marking the extension of the forests; and stretching along the base of the range a broad belt of rose-purple; all these colors, from the blue sky to the yellow valley smoothly blending as they do in a rainbow, making a wall of light ineffably fine. Then it seemed to me that the Sierra should be called, not the Nevada or Snowy Range, but the Range of Light. And after ten years of wandering and wondering in the heart of it, rejoicing in its glorious floods of light, the white beams of the morning streaming through the passes, the noonday radiance on the crystal rocks, the flush of the alpenglow, and the irised spray of countless waterfalls, it still seems above all others the Range of Light.

JOHN MUIR (1838–1914), a naturalist and early advocate of environmental conservation, was largely responsible for the establishment of both Yosemite and Sequoia National Parks. This extract describes Muir's first trip to Yosemite, including his famous observations on the light of the Sierra Mountains.

The Spectacle of the Falls

During the time of the spring floods the best near view of the fall is obtained from Fern Ledge on the east side above the blinding spray at a height of about four hundred feet above the base of the fall. A climb of about fourteen hundred feet from the valley has to be made, and there is no trail, but to any one fond of climbing this will make the ascent all the more delightful. A narrow part of the ledge extends to the side of the fall and back of it, enabling us to approach it as closely as we wish. When the afternoon sunshine is streaming through the throng of comets, ever wasting, ever renewed, the marvelous fineness, firmness, and variety of their forms are beautifully revealed. At the top of the fall they seem to burst forth in irregular spurts from some grand, throbbing mountain-heart. Now and then one mighty throb sends forth a mass of solid water into the free air far beyond the others, which rushes alone to the bottom of the fall with long streaming tail, like combed silk, while the others, descending in clusters, gradually mingle and lose their identity. But they all rush past us with amazing velocity and display of power, though apparently drowsy and deliberate in their movements when observed from a distance of a mile or two. The heads of these comet-like masses are composed of nearly solid water, and are dense white in color like pressed snow, from the friction they suffer in rushing through the air, the portion worn off forming the tail, between the white lustrous threads and films of which faint, grayish pencilings appear, while the outer, finer sprays of water-dust, whirling in sunny eddies, are pearly gray throughout. At the bottom of the fall there is but little distinction of form visible. It is mostly a hissing, clashing, seething, upwhirling mass of scud and spray, through which the light sifts in gray and purple tones, while at times when the sun strikes at the required angle, the whole wild and apparently lawless, stormy, striving mass is changed to brilliant rainbow hues, manifesting finest harmony. The middle portion of the fall is the most openly beautiful; lower, the various forms into which the waters are wrought are more closely and voluminously veiled, while higher, toward the head, the current is comparatively simple and undivided. But even at the bottom, in the boiling clouds of spray, there is no confusion, while the rainbow light makes all divine, adding glorious beauty and peace to

In Mariposa Grove, Yosemite Park, some of the giant trees with heights of over 70 metres (227 feet) almost seem to touch the sky. Next to them the spruce look tiny.

Redwood National Park is located on the north coast of California. The damp, relatively cool climate is ideal for the ferns growing here to abundance.

glorious power. This noble fall has far the richest, as well as the most powerful, voice of all the falls of the valley, its tones varying from the sharp hiss and rustle of the wind in the glossy leaves of the Live-oaks and the soft, sifting, hushing tones of the Pines, to the loudest rush and roar of storm-winds and thunder among the crags of the summit peaks. The low bass, booming, reverberating tones, heard under favorable circumstances five or six miles away, are formed by the dashing and exploding of heavy masses mixed with air upon two projecting ledges on the face of the cliff, the one on which we are standing and another about two hundred feet above it. The torrent of massive comets is continuous at time of high water, while the explosive, booming notes are wildly intermittent, because, unless influenced by the wind, most of the heavier masses shoot out from the face of the precipice, and pass the ledges upon which at other times they are exploded. Occasionally the whole fall is swayed away from the front of the cliff, then suddenly dashed flat against it, or vibrated from side to side like a pendulum, giving rise to endless variety of forms and sounds.

JOHN MUIR worked at several jobs during his stay in Yosemite. In 1869 – 1870, he worked for James Hutchings, the first permanent resident of the valley, building and then operating a sawmill. At was at this time that Muir first encountered Yosemite Falls.

Respect for the Redwoods

The redwoods, once seen, leave a mark or create a vision that stays with you always. No one has ever successfully painted or photographed a redwood tree. The feeling they produce is not transferable. From them comes silence an awe. It's not only their unbelievable stature, nor the color which seems to shift and vary under your eyes, no, they are not like any trees we know, they are ambassadors from another time. They have the mystery of ferns that disappeared a million years ago into the coal of the carboniferous era. They carry their own light and shade. The vainest, most slap-happy and irreverent of men, in the presence of redwoods, goes under a spell of wonder and respect. Respect – that's the word. One feels the need to bow to unquestioned sovereigns. I have known these great ones since my earliest childhood, have lived among them, camped and slept against their warm monster bodies, and no amount of association has bred contempt in me. …

Left: The hollow trunk of a sequoia, with space enough for a spruce to grow inside.

Right: Redwoods go on living even when their trunks, as sometimes happens, become hollow.

The trees rise straight up to zenith; there is no horizon. The dawn comes early and remains dawn until the sun is high. Then the green fernlike foliage so far up strains the sunlight to a green gold and distributes it in shafts or rather in stripes of light and shade. After the sun passes zenith it is afternoon and quickly evening with a whispering dusk as long as was the morning.

Thus time and the ordinary divisions of the day are changed. To me dawn and dusk are quiet times, and here in the redwoods nearly the whole of daylight is a quiet time. Birds move in the dim light or flash like sparks through the stripes of sun, but they make little sound. Underfoot is a mattress of needles deposited for over two thousand years. No sound of footsteps can be heard on this thick blanket. To me there's a remote and cloistered feeling here. One holds back speech for fear of disturbing something – what? From my earliest childhood I've felt that something was going on in the groves, something of which I was not a part. And if I had forgotten the feeling, I soon got it back.

At night, the darkness is black – only straight up a patch of gray and an occasional star. And there's a breathing in the black, for these huge things that control the day and inhabit the night are living things and have presence, and perhaps feeling, and, somewhere in deep-down perception, perhaps communication I have had lifelong association with these things. (Odd that the word "trees" does not apply.) I can accept them and their power and their age because I was early exposed to them. On the other hand, people lacking such experience begin to have a feeling of uneasiness here, of danger, of being shut in, enclosed and overwhelmed. It is not only the size of these redwoods but their strangeness that frightens them. And why not? For these are the last remaining members of a race that flourished over four continents as far back in geologic time as the upper Jurassic period. Fossils of these ancients have been found dating from the Cretaceous era while in the Eocene and Miocene they were spread over England and Europe and America. And then the glaciers moved down and wiped the Titans out beyond recovery. And only these few are left – a stunning memory of what the world was like once long ago. Can it be that we do not love to be reminded that we are very young and callow in a world that was old when we came into it? And could there be a strong resistance to the certainty that a

The Ancient Bristlecone Pine Forest features a tree shaped like a bizarre sculpture. No other trees grow at this height . . .

living world will continue its stately way when we no longer inhabit it?

Nobel Prize-winner JOHN STEINBECK (1902 – 1968) found the redwoods of his native California to be unique and full of mystique. The trees appeared as artifacts of antiquity, filling observers with awe and wonder and commanding respect.

Song of the Redwood

A California song,

A prophecy and indirection, a thought impalpable to breathe as air,

A chorus of dryads, fading, departing, or hamadryads departing,

A murmuring, fateful, giant voice, out of the earth and sky,

Voice of a mighty dying tree in the redwood forest dense. . . .

Along the northern coast,

Just back from the rock-bound shore and the caves,

In the saline air from the sea in the Mendocino country,

With the surge for base and accompaniment low and hoarse,

With crackling blows of axes sounding musically driven by strong arms,

Riven deep by the sharp tongues of the axes, there in the redwood forest dense,

I heard the mighty tree its death-chant chanting.

The choppers heard not, the camp shanties echoed not,

The quick-car'd teamsters and chain and jack-screw men heard not,

As the wood-spirits came from their haunts of a thousand years to join the refrain,

But in my soul I plainly heard.

Murmuring out of its myriad leaves,

Down from its lofty top rising two hundred feet high,

Out of its stalwart trunk and limbs, out of its foot-thick bark,

That chant of the seasons and time, chant not of the past only but the future. . . .

Then to a loftier strain,

Still prouder, more ecstatic rose the chant,

As if the heirs, the deities of the West,

Joining with master-tongue bore part. . . .

In the echo of teamsters' calls and the clinking chains, and the music of choppers' axes,

. . . under these extreme climatic conditions, this member of the pine family grows very slowly, but can, on the other hand, live for up to 4,000 years.

The falling trunk and limbs, the crash, the muffled shriek, the groan,

Such words combined from the redwood-tree, as of voices ecstatic, ancient and rustling,

The century-lasting, unseen dryads, singing, withdrawing,

All their recesses of forests and mountains leaving,

From the Cascade range to the Wahsatch, or Idaho far, or Utah,

To the deities of the modern henceforth yielding,

The chorus and indications, the vistas of coming humanity, the settlements, features all,

In the Mendocino woods I caught.

WALT WHITMAN (1819 – 1892) was a revolutionary figure in nineteenth century American literature. This poem is taken from his collection "Leaves of Grass". It expresses wholehearted optimism for the "new" society but also a little regret at the downfall of the existing way of life.

The Sequoias

One of my own best excursions among the Sequoias was made in the autumn of 1875, when I explored the then unknown or little known Sequoia region south of the Mariposa Grove for comprehensive views of the belt, and to learn what I could of the peculiar distribution of the species and its history in general. In particular I was anxious to try to find out whether it had ever been more widely distributed since the glacial period; what conditions favorable or otherwise were affecting it; what were its relations to climate, topography, soil, and the other trees growing with it, etc.; and whether, as was generally supposed, the species was nearing extinction. I was already acquainted in a general way with the northern groves, but excepting some passing glimpses gained on excursions into the High Sierra about the head-waters of King's and Kern Rivers I had seen nothing of the south end of the belt.

Nearly all my mountaineering has been done on foot, carrying as little as possible, depending on camp-fires for warmth, that so I might be light and free to go wherever my studies might lead. On this Sequoia trip, which promised to be long, I was persuaded to take a small wild mule with me to carry provisions and a pair of blankets. The friendly owner of the animal, having noticed that I sometimes looked tired when I came down from the peaks to replenish my bread-sack, assured me that his "little

Brownie mule" was just what I wanted, tough as a knot, perfectly untirable, low and narrow, just right for squeezing through brush, able to climb like a chipmunk, jump from boulder to boulder like a wild sheep, and go anywhere a man could go. But tough as he was and accomplished as a climber, many a time in the course of our journey when he was jaded and hungry, wedged fast in rocks or struggling in chaparral like a fly in a spiderweb, his troubles were sad to see, and I wished he would leave me and find his way home alone.

We set out from Yosemite about the end of August and our first camp was made in the well-known Mariposa Grove. Here and in the adjacent Pine woods I spent nearly a week, carfully examining the boundaries of the grove for traces of its greater extension without finding any. Then I struck out into the majestic trackless forest to the southeastward, hoping to find new groves or traces of old ones in the dense Silver Fir and Pine woods about the head of Big Creek, where soil and climate seemed most favorable to their growth, but not a single tree or old monument of any sort came to light until I climbed the high rock called Wamellow by the Indians. Here I obtained telling views of the fertile forest-filled basin of the upper Fresno. Innumerable spires of the noble Yellow Pine were displayed rising above one another on the braided slopes, and yet nobler Sugar Pines with superb arms outstretched in the rich autumn light, while away toward the southwest, on the verge of the glowing horizon, I discovered the majestic dome-like crowns of Big Trees towering high over all, singly and in close grove congregations. There is something wonderfully attractive in this king tree, even when beheld from afar, that draws us to it with indescribable enthusiasm; its superior height and massive smoothly rounded outlines proclaiming its character in any company; and when one of the oldest attains full stature on some commanding ridge it seems the very god of the woods. ...

The Fresno Big Trees covered an area of about four square miles, and while wandering about surveying the boundaries of the grove, anxious to see every tree, I came suddenly on a handsome log cabin, richly embowered and so fresh and unweathered it was still redolent of gum and balsam like a newly felled tree. Strolling forward, wondering who could have built it, I found an old, weary-eyed, speculative, gray-haired man on a bark stool by the door, reading a book. The discovery of his hermitage by a stranger seemed to surprise him, but when I explained that I was only a tree-lover sauntering along the mountains to study Sequoia, he bade me welcome, made me

bring my mule down to a little slanting meadow before his door and camp with him, promising to show me his pet trees and many curious things bearing on my studies.

After supper, as the evening shadows were falling, the good hermit sketched his life in the mines, which in the main was like that of most other pioneer gold-hunters – a succession of intense experiences full of big ups and downs like the mountain topography. ... The name of my hermit friend is John A. Nelder, a fine kind man, who in going into the woods has at last gone home; for he loves nature truly, and realizes that these last shadowy days with scarce a glint of gold in them are the best of all. Birds, squirrels, plants get loving, natural recognition, and delightful it was to see how sensitively he responds to the silent influences of the woods. His eyes brightened as he gazed on the trees that stand guard around his little home; squirrels and mountain quail came to his call to be fed, and he tenderly stroked the little snow-bent sapling Sequoias, hoping they yet might grow straight to the sky and rule the grove. ...

Down into the main King's River cañon, a mile deep, I led and dragged and shoved my patient, much-enduring mule through miles and miles of gardens and brush, fording innumerable streams, crossing savage rock slopes and taluses, scrambling, sliding through gulches and gorges, then up into the grand Sequoia forests of the south side, cheered by the royal crowns displayed on the narrow horizon. In a day and a half we reached the Sequoia woods in the neighborhood of the old Thomas' Mill Flat. Thence striking off northeastward I found a magnificent forest nearly six miles long by two in width, composed mostly of Big Trees, with outlying groves as far east as Boulder Creek. Here five or six days were spent, and it was delightful to learn from countless trees, old and young, how comfortably they were settled down in concordance with climate and soil and their noble neighbors.

Imbedded in these majestic woods there are numerous meadows, around the sides of which the Big Trees press close together in beautiful lines, showing their grandeur openly from the ground to their domed heads in the sky. The young trees are still more numerous and exuberant than in the Fresno and Dinky groves, standing apart in beautiful family groups, or crowding around the old giants. For every venerable lightning-stricken tree, there is one or more in all the glory of prime, and for each of these, many young trees and crowds of saplings. The young trees express the grandeur of their race in a way indefinable by any words at my command. When

Moro Rock, 2,050 metres (6,662 feet) high, towers above the canyons of Sequoia National Park. It is easy to climb and offers a splendid view of the surrounding countryside from the top.

A ghostly waterscape: Mono Lake with its bizarre pillars of calc-tufa.

they are five or six feet in diameter and a hundred and fifty feet high, they seem like mere baby saplings as many inches in diameter, their juvenile habit and gestures completely veiling their real size, even to those who from long experience, are able to make fair approximation in their measurements of common trees. One morning I noticed three airy, spiry, quickgrowing babies on the side of a meadow, the largest of which I took to be about eight inches in diameter. On measuring it, I found to my astonishment it was five feet six inches in diameter, and about a hundred and forty feet high. ...

A short distance south of this forest lies a beautiful grove, now mostly included in the General Grant National Park. I found many shake-makers at work in it, access to these magnificient woods having been made easy to be the old mill wagon road. The Park is only two miles square, and the largest of its many fine trees is the General Grant, so named before the date of my first visit, twenty-eight years ago, and said to be the largest tree in the world, though above the craggy bulging base the diameter is less than thirty feet. The Sanger Lumber Company owns nearly all the King's River groves outside the Park, and for many years the mills have been spreading desolation without any advantage. ...

I found a scattered growth of Big Trees extending across the main divide to within a short distance of Hyde's Mill, on a tributary of Dry Creek. The mountain ridge on the south side of the stream was covered from base to summit with a most superb growth of Big Trees. What a picture it made! In all my wide forest wanderings I had seen none so sublime. Every tree of all the mighty host seemed perfect in beauty and strength, and their majestic domed heads, rising above one another on the mountain slope, were most imposingly displayed, like a range of bossy upswelling cumulus clouds on a calm sky.

In this glorious forest the mill was busy, forming a sore, sad center of destruction though small as yet, so immensely heavy was the growth. Only the smaller and most accessible of the trees were being cut. The logs, from three to ten or twelve feet in diameter, were dragged or rolled with long strings of oxen into a chute and sent flying down the steep mountain-side to the mill flat, where the largest of them were blasted into manageable dimensions for the saws. And as the timber is very brash, by this blasting and careless felling on uneven ground, half or three fourths of the timber was wasted.

I spent several days exploring the ridge and counting the annual wood-rings on a large number of stumps in the clearings, then replenished my bread-sack and pushed on southward. All the way across the broad rough basins of the Kaweah and Tule River Sequoia ruled supreme, forming an almost continuous belt for sixty or seventy miles, waving up and down in huge massy mountain-billows in compliance with the grand glacier-ploughed topography.

The redwood is commonly referred to as the sequoia, named after the Indian chief Sequoyah. JOHN MUIR began in 1875 to study the Sierra sequoias, following the Yosemite Valley to the Kern Basin, a distance of over two hundred miles.

The Ouzel and Other Birds

The waterfalls of the Sierra are frequented by only one bird – the ouzel or water thrush *(Cinclus Mexicanus, Sw.)*. He is a singularly joyous and lovable little fellow, about the size of a robin, clad in a plain waterproof suit of bluish gray, with a tinge of chocolate on the head and shoulders. In form he is about as smoothly plump and compact as a pebble that had been whirled in a pot-hole, the flowing contour of his body being interrupted only by his strong feet and bill, the crisp wing-tips, and the upslanted wren-like tail.

Among all the countless waterfalls I have met in the course of ten years' exploration in the Sierra, whether among the icy peaks, or warm foot-hills, or in the profound yosemitic cañons of the middle region, not one was found without its ouzel. No cañon is too cold for this little bird, none too lonely, provided it be rich in falling water. Find a fall, or cascade, or rushing rapid, anywhere upon a clear stream, and there you will surely find its complementary ouzel, flitting about in the spray, diving in foaming eddies, whirling like a leaf among beaten foam-bells; ever vigorous and enthusiastic, yet self-contained, and neither seeking nor shunning your company.

One wild winter morning, when Yosemite Valley was swept its length from west to east by a cordial snowstorm, I sallied forth to see what I might learn and enjoy. A sort of gray, gloaming-like darkness filled the valley, the huge walls were out of sight, all ordinary sounds were smothered, and even the loudest booming of the falls was at times buried beneath the roar of the heavy-laden blast. The loose snow was already over five feet deep on the meadows, making extended walks impossible without the aid of snowshoes. I found no great difficulty, however, in making my way to a certain ripple on the river where one of my ouzels lived. He was at home, busily gleaning his breakfast among the

Zabriskie Point in Death Valley. The barren, lifeless landscape is dominated by the peak of Manly Beacon.

Panoramic views of Death Valley. Above: Racetrack Valley. Below: The view from Zabriskie Point.

pebbles of a shallow portion of the margin, apparently unaware of anything extraordinary in the weather. Presently he flew out to a stone against which the icy current was beating, and turning his back to the wind, sang as delightfully as a lark in springtime.

After spending an hour or two with my favorite, I made my way across the valley, boring and wallowing through the drifts, to learn as definitely as possible how the other birds were spending their time. The Yosemite birds are easily found during the winter because all of them excepting the ouzel are restricted to the sunny north side of the valley, the south side being constantly eclipsed by the great frosty shadow of the wall. And because the Indian Cañon groves, from their peculiar exposure are the warmest, the birds congregate there, more especially in severe weather.

I found most of the robins cowering on the lee side of the larger branches where the snow could not fall upon them, while two of three of the more enterprising were making desperate efforts to reach the mistletoe berries by clinging nervously to the under side of the snow-crowned masses, back downward, like woodpeckers. Every now and then they would dislodge some of the loose fringes of the snow-crown, which would come sifting down on them and send them screaming back to camp, where they would subside among their companions with a shiver, muttering in low, querulous chatter like hungry children. Some of the sparrows were busy at the feet of larger trees gleaning seeds and benumbed insects, joined now and then by a robin weary of his unsuccsessful attempts upon the snow-covered berries. The brave woodpeckers were clinging to the snowless sides of the larger boles and overarching branches of the camp trees, making short flights from side to side of the grove, pecking now and then at the acorns they had stored in the bark, and chartering aimlessly as if unable to keep still, yet evidently putting in the time in a very dull way, like storm-bound travelers at a country tavern. The hardy nuthatches were threading the open furrows of the trunks in their usual industrious manner, and uttering their quaint notes, evidently less distressed than their neighbors. The Steller's jays were, of course, making more noisy stir than all the other birds combined; ever coming and going with loud bluster, screaming as if each had a lump of melting sludge in his throat, and taking good care to improve the favorable opportunity afforded by the storm to steal from the acorn stores of the woodpeckers. I also noticed one solitary gray eagle braving the storm on the top of a

tall Pine stump just outside the main grove. He was standing bolt upright with his back to the wind, a tuft of snow piled on his square shoulders, a monument of passive endurance. Thus every snow-bound bird seemed more or less uncomfortable if not in positive distress. The storm was reflected in every gesture, and not one cheerful note, not to say song, came from a single bill; their cowering, joyless endurance offering a striking contrast to the spontaneous, irrepressible gladness of the ouzel, who could no more help exhaling sweet song than a rose sweet fragrance. He *must* sing, though the heavens fall. I remember noticing the distress of a pair of robins during the violent earthquake of the year 1872, when the Pines of the valley, with strange movements, flapped and waved their branches, and beetling rock brows came thundering down to the meadows in tremendous avalanches. It did not occur to me in the midst of the excitement of other observations to look for the ouzels, but I doubt not they were singing straight on through it all, regarding the terrible rock thunder as fearlessly as they do the booming of the waterfalls.

During his travels through the California wilderness, JOHN MUIR also studied the water ouzel and many other birds.

Desecration of a Wilderness

The first time I visited Yosemite National Park was in August 1944. The crowds were small, the waterfalls dry, and the hitchhiking tough. Since then everything I've heard and read about Yosemite has made it seem less and less worth returning to. But I went back for a big weekend recently to see for myself. Things are not as bad there as I'd expected; I was disappointed.

In the foothills of the Sierras, up through the old mining towns like Coulterville and Chinese Camp, the flowers were blooming – silverleaf lupine, California poppy, paintbrush and penstemon – and the traffic seemed light. When we saw a sign, Water Ahead, I looked forward to a drink of pure Sierra Nevada spring water, fresh from the rocks. We found the spring, but another sign beside it said, Water Contaminated – Unfit to Drink. Well, that was more like it. But getting into the park was easy. Instead of the traffic jam I expected, we found only two cars in front of us at Big Oak Flat and I was surprised when the ranger-cashier in the box office said that Yosemite Valley was already full. I wished him a Happy Easter and he rolled his eyes heavenward.

Somewhere near Cascade Creek we stopped at a turnout for the classic view of Yosemite Valley, as invented by Ansel Adams. There was El Capitan, Half

The twisted salt formations of the Devil's Golf Course in Death Valley. Such a course could only be of the devil's devising.

Death Valley. The Sand Dunes start at the southern end of Mesquite Flat.

In addition to the Joshua tree, the cholla cactus is another familiar feature of Joshua Tree National Monument.

Dome, Sentinel Dome, Bridalveil Falls, and a blue haze above the valley floor. Woodsmoke? Exhaust fumes? The friend with me remarked that she thought Bridalveil a nice name for a waterfall. Two long-haired boys went by, walking their bicycles up the grade. Looking hard, I found my first Budweiser can below the bridge, down in the clear snow water. I clumbered down the slippery granite in my dude boots, not to retrieve the can – *Let Nature Alone* – but for a drink of real mountain water. Spray paint on the boulders read, Joe & Juanita Was Here 7-4-70, and, Running Bear 1851. . . .

The people at park headquarters were helpful and hospitable when I appeared to investigate their law-enforcement practices. "We have nothing to hide," said Staff Park Ranger Richard Marks. . . .

Ranger Tom Wylle, supervisor of the night shift, took me along on three of his patrols. In a car, of course – horses are used only for trail work now and . . . cavalry maneuvers. . . .

For two hours we cruise through the campgrounds, in and out of parking lots, around the drives. Wylie straightens out a campsite mixup, which involves a great deal of paperwork and radio exchanges. He speaks quietly to a hairy young man walking the street with a bottle of wine in his hand, sends him back to his campsite. The freak offers us peanuts from a poke; we eat some of his peanuts. Ten in the evening, beginning of campground "quiet time." The air is foggy with the smoke from 500 campfires, rich with the dreamy redolence of *Cannabis sativa.* Sounds of music and jubilation – Wylie has to caution the party against excessive noise. Others are trying to sleep, he reminds them, and indeed, all around us, we can see through the gloom and the trees the pale forms of pickup campers, camper trailers, and Winnebago motor homes, where Middle America is bedding down to another night of lawful conjugal bliss. . . .

We pause at headquarters to check the prisoners in the jail. Oh yes, Yosemite National Park has its own tidy little jail, which I inspected. I've seen worse; I've been in worse. For temporary custody only; no one is kept there more than a day or two. The park also has its own resident U. S. commissioner to administer the law. How escape it? On a typical summer weekend there may be anywhere from 20,000 to 30,000 people in and out of Yosemite Valley. It's a small city much of the year, but one in which the population is permanently transient, always changing. Which

Death Valley. In the background, the dried-up lake known as Racetrack Valley. The name of the area is deceptive: even Death Valley has its communities of plants and animals adapted to the climate.

makes things even harder for the ranger-cops. They never have a chance to get to know the people they police except as types and stereotypes: as "hippies", "straights," "average families." The average family has 2.4 children; the freak familiy may have from 10 to 500. How to deal with them? ...

I was shown the records and statistics. In 1952 the Yosemite district had 55 "cases" of illegal activity: in 1958 there were 182, mostly traffic violations; in 1970 the record shows 765 cases, with a total of 2,170 persons charged with various offenses, among them 92 for disorderly conduct, 13 as "run-aways", 648 for larceny, 16 for auto thefts, 1 for rape, 2 for manslaughter, 2 for robbery, 24 for aggravated assault, 29 for burglary, 62 for narcotics, 34 for drunkenness, and 106 for "soliciting" (begging and hitchhiking). Of the 765 cases, 564 involved juveniles. That's life in the woods in Yosemite Valley. To handle this happy holiday scene, the Park Service employs seven permanent rangers in Yosemite Valley plus thirty to thirty-five summer seasonals, most of them without training in police work.

Perhaps the banning of private cars from Yosemite Valley will reduce the crime problem. Perhaps not. Probably not if the private cars are simply replaced by a mass transit system. For the basic trouble here is urbanism. Yosemite Valley has been urbanized. It's no more a wild or natural area than Manhattan's Central Park. ...

The Park Service believes that Yosemite Valley is not the proper location for youth festivals, organized or disorganized. No doubt true. (The frogs, having an orgiastic celebration of their own, might not agree.) But I can think of other things that Yosemite Valley is not the proper place for. It is not the proper place for paved roads and motor traffic in any form. It is not the proper place for gas stations, supermarkets, bars, curio shops, barbershops, a hospital, a lodge, a hotel, a convention center, and a small city of permanent and transient residents. Above all Yosemite Valley is not a proper place for a jail, for administrators, for police wearing park ranger uniforms. ...

On my last night in Yosemite I walked alone through the meadows and listened to the bellowing frogs, maddened with moonlight. Out of a notch in the granite cliff I could see Yosemite Falls, the extravagant gush of milky foam dropping 1,400 feet through space, dissolving in mist, regrouping in cascades below to fall 600 feet more to the valley floor. Through the inner smog of figures and problems I dimly imagined Yosemite as it must have been in 1851 when Chief Tenaya and his little band of renegades were driven out. (Renegades: Indians unwilling to camp in officially designated campsites.) No wonder they hid and fought and escaped and fought again and wept and died. Yosemite Valley was a wild, savage, splendid and precious place then. …

What should Yosemite Valley be? It should be what it once was; the kind of place where a person would know himself lucky to make one pilgrimage there in his lifetime. A holy place.

Keep it like it was.

EDWARD ABBEY is a keen conservationist. In this extract, Abbey records his dismay at the tourism which has developed in Yosemite Valley. Abbey had first visited the area in the 1940s, and returned over thirty years later.

The Valley of the Sacramento

We were now in the valley of plenty. Our poor teeth, which had been laboring on the filelike consistency of pilot bread, had now a respite, in the agreeable task of masticating from the 'flesh pots' of California.

As we determined to lay over during the day, our wagon master, Traverse, concluded to butcher an ox, and the hungry Arabs of our train were regaled with a feast of dead kine. Feeling an aristocratic longing for a rich beef steak, I determined to have one. There was not a particle of fat in the steak to make gravy, nor was there a slice of bacon to be had to fry it with, and the flesh was as dry and as hard as a bone. But a nice broiled steak, with a plenty of gravy, I would have – and I had it. The inventive genius of an emigrant is almost constantly called forth on the plains, and so in my case, I laid a nice cut on the coals, which, instead of broiling, only burnt and carbonized like a piece of wood, and when one side was turned to cinder, I whopped it over to make charcoal of the other. To make butter gravy, I melted a stearin candle, which I poured over the delicious tit-bit, and, smacking my lips, sat down to my feast, the envy of several lookers-on. I sopped the first mouthful in the nice looking gravy, and put it between my teeth, when the gravy cooled almost instantly, and the roof of my mouth and my teeth were coated all over with a covering like hard beeswax, making mastication next to impossible.

'How does it go?' asked one.

'O, first rate,' said I, struggling to get hard, dry morsel down my throat; and cutting another piece, which was free from the delicious gravy, 'Come, try it,' said I; 'I have more than I can eat (which was true). You are welcome to it.' The envious, hungry soul sat down and, putting a large piece between his teeth, after rolling it about in his mouth awhile, deliberately spit it out, saying, with an oath, that

'Chips and beeswax are hard fare, even for a starving man.'

Ah, how hard words and want of sentiment will steal over one's better nature on the plains. As for the rest of the steak, we left it to choke the wolves.

ALONZO DELANO was advised by his doctor that a journey across the plains would benefit his health. He set off from St. Joseph, Missouri, for California in 1849. It was the height of the Gold Rush and Delano intended to sell goods to the miners.

A Quiet Drive

We left Sacramento at dawn and were crossing the Nevada desert by noon, after a hurling passage of the Sierras that made the fag and the tourists cling to each other in the back seat. We were in front, we took over. Dean was happy again. All he needed was a wheel in his hand and four on the road. He talked about how bad a driver Old Bull Lee was and to demonstrate – 'Whenever a huge big truck like that one coming loomed into sight it would take Bull infinite time to spot it, 'cause he couldn't see, man, he can't *see*.' He rubbed his eyes furiously to show. 'And I'd say, "Whoop, look out, Bull, a truck", and he'd say, "Eh? what's that you say, Dean?" "Truck! truck!" and at the *very* last *moment* he would go right up to the truck like this –' And Dean hurled the Plymouth head-on at the truck roaring our way, wobbled and hovered in front of it a moment, the truck driver's face growing grey before our eyes, the people in the back seat subsiding in gasps of horror, and swung away at the last moment. 'Like that, you see, exactly like that, how bad he was.' I wasn't scared at all; I knew Dean. The people in the back seat were speechless. In fact they were afraid to complain: God knew what Dean would do, they thought, if they should ever complain. He balled right across the desert in this manner, demonstrating various ways of how not to drive, how his father used to drive jalopies, how great drivers made curves, how bad drivers move over too far in the beginning and had to scramble at the curve's end and so on. It was a hot, sunny afternoon.

With his novel On the Road, *JACK KEROUAC (1922 – 1969) inspired a generation to take to the highways of America. Although published as fiction, the work is based on the author's experiences.*

The splendid flower of a "sword tree" in the Mojave Desert. The plant is well protected by its hard, sharp-edged leaves.

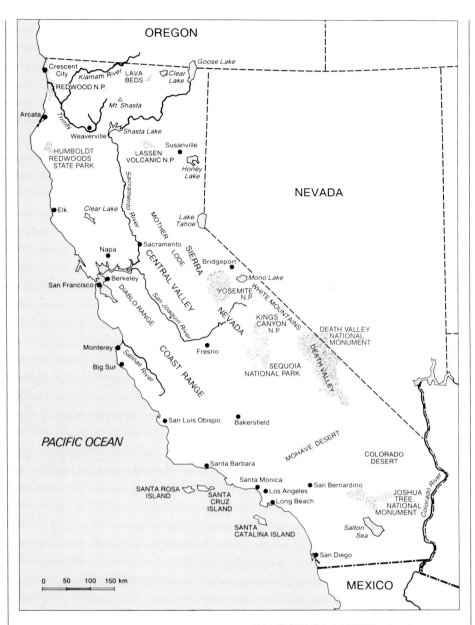

THE PLANT WORLD

BIGELOW CHOLLA, a species of cactus which stores water in its stem and stalks; its roots are close to the earth's surface so that the little rain that does fall can easily be absorbed. There are no leaves, only spines which protect the plant from the sun and animals. The cholla is found throughout the desert regions.

BIG LEAF MAPLE, also called Oregon maple, a maple tree with large leaves growing to heights of 30 metres (97 feet); famous for a beautiful autumn colouring. The big leaves are the characteristic feature of this tree, and the seeds are so shaped that they spin to earth like helicopters.

CALIFORNIA LAUREL, also known as myrtlewood. The evergreen laurel is recognized by its characteristic smell.

CALIFORNIA RED FIR, a conifer growing between 1,800 and 3,000 metres (5,850 – 9,750 feet) above sea level in the mountains of Yosemite National Park. One of the characteristic features of this symmetrically-formed tree is its thick, deeply fissured bark, dark red on the outside and light red inside.

CAT'S CLAW. A type of acacia which grows in places sheltered from strong winds. As a tree, it can grow up to 4 metres (13 feet) tall, but otherwise appears as a very low spreading bush.

CHOLLA CACTUS, a very beautiful type of cactus with numerous spines growing in Joshua Tree National Monument.

CREOSOTE BUSH, a bush with deep, wide-spreading roots enabling it to absorb the maximum amount of water.

DESERT CALICO, a plant belonging to the phlox (*polemoniacea*) family, with very small pink flowers.

DESERT WILLOW, also known as desert catalpa, usually growing near water or in the bed of small streams. It has very deep roots in order to extract moisture from the sandy soil.

DOUGLAS FIR. The best known of all the Pacific Ocean trees, this fir was named after the Scottish botanist David Douglas. It is recognized by its long, coarse needles, and, with a firm red core, is a valuable timber often used for construction.

INDIGO BUSH, a shrub well adapted to desert conditions, found in Joshua Tree National Monument. From April to May, it bears purple flowers.

JEFFREY PINE, a highly robust pine growing at heights of between 1,000 and 3,000 metres (3,250 – 9,750 feet) above sea level. The fissured, red-brown bark gives off a powerful vanilla or pineapple aroma.

JOJOBA, Joshua Tree National Monument: a plant bearing oily nuts highly valued as a source of nutrition by the Indians and today used in the cosmetic industry.

JOSHUA TREE, a yucca palm which belongs to the agave family. Leathery leaves protect it from drying up in the heat, providing shelter for many different species of birds.

JUNIPER, the California juniper grows in the higher regions of the Mojave Desert and is well adapted to the barren surroundings. Animals feed on its fruit.

LODGEPOLE PINE, a massive variety of pine which is resistant to the harsh climatic conditions prevailing at heights of 2,100 to 3,000 metres (6,825 – 9,750 feet) above sea level. The Indians used these trees to build their homes, hence the name given to the structures.

MESQUITE. The roots of this member of the acacia family reach deep into the

covering the branches provides protection from excessive evaporation. This shrub is particularly beautiful in spring, when it is covered by blossoms.

PALO VERDE, occurs in various sizes, from a small bush to a tree; its tiny leaves are shed shortly after the rainy

QUAKING ASPEN, a species growing along water courses in the higher areas of Yosemite National Park, frequently in sandy soil.

RED ALDER, usually to be found along water ways and damp valleys. A deciduous tree, its characteristic features

Ancient Bristolcone Pine Forest.

earth extracting the large quantities of water it needs to survive. Its fruit is used as animal fodder.

NOLINA, a type of thick trunked yucca palm with spiny, fleshy leaves and cream-coloured flowers.

OCOTILLO PATCH, a desert plant growing in the Pinto Basin with spines like a cactus; it is in fact a foliate shrub belonging to the ocotillo family. During long dry periods, it sheds its leaves to conserve water but its bark continues to grow. To protect it from further moisture loss, the trunk of the plant is under the earth, leaving only the tips of the branches exposed. The layer of resin

season. The chlorophyll in the trunk and branches gives it its green colouring and absorbs the light energy necessary for the conversion of carbon dioxide and water into carbohydrates.

PARKER GROUP, Sequoia National Park. This cluster of tall trees was named after the family of Captain Parker, superintendent of Sequoia National Park from 1893 to 1894.

PINYON TREE, a dwarf pine with a short trunk and spreading crown; a conifer which is able to withstand extreme heat.

The **PURPLE MAT** belongs to the *hydrophyllaceae* family: a creeping plant with very small pink flowers.

are broad leaves, cones and a silver-grey bark.

REDWOODS. In an area extending from Placer County west of Lake Tahoe to Tulare County east of Visalia, the Sierra Redwood is the native species; it is concentrated in groves on the west side of the Sierra Nevadas, at heights between 1,500 and 2,500 metres (5,625 to 9,345 feet). The Coast Redwood grows in the California Coast Range, in the area between southwest Oregon and the southern border of Monterey County formed by the Santa Lucia Mountains. The Dawn Redwood, introduced from central China, loses its needles once a year; it only grows in the coastal area between Oregon and Monterey County, frequently reaching a height of over 80 metres (260 feet). Its roots go down less than two metres (6 feet) into the ground. The average circumference of the redwood is almost 5 metres (16 feet). Redwoods take 500 years to reach their full height.

SITKA SPRUCE, grows on the west coast approximately at sea level; it is around 60 metres (195 feet) tall, has very spiny evergreen needles and rather long cones. The light weight of the wood makes it an excellent material for aircraft construction.

SMOKE TREE, a large bush belonging to the pea family. It is only when there are floods, causing the movement of rocks, that the hard shell of the seed is burst so that it is able to germinate.

SPRING FLOWERS. The seeds of over 700 different types of desert flower, germinating only after a period of rain, transform the desert into a sea of colour. Before the flowers wilt, new seeds are formed which lie dormant until the next fall of rain washes away their protective layer, allowing new flowers to grow.

WASHINGTON PALM, also known as the fan palm, only grows in places where there is an adequate water supply, be it fresh or salt water. These palms mark the course of the San Andreas Fault, since the displacement of the rocks dammed up the ground water, causing it to rise to the surface.

The **WESTERN HEMLOCK** reaches heights of up to 50 metres (162 feet) and is recognized by its bent-over top.

WESTERN WHITE PINE, a well-known pine that is very common in California, growing in high altitudes up to the tree line.

WHITE FIR grows tallest in fertile ground, but is sufficiently hardy to survive at altitudes between 1,500 and 2,400 metres (5,625–7,800 feet) above sea level. It has either a white or silver bark.

THE ANIMAL WORLD

BADGER. The badger hunts reptiles and rodents by digging in the ground with its strong front paws; it sleeps in burrows in the daytime and is very active at night when the temperature is cooler.

BAT. This animal only hunts for its food during the hours from dusk to dawn. It feeds on insects and lives in crevices in the rocks, sheltered from the sun and the wind.

BEECHEY GROUND SQUIRREL. Instead of drinking, this squirrel obtains all the water it needs from the seeds it eats. It has adapted to the desert climate by hibernating during the summer.

BIGHORN SHEEP. This breed of sheep only needs to drink every few days and through this economical use of water, it is better able to withstand the heat. It eats only the parts of the plants that are its food, enabling the plant to rejuvenate itself rather easily.

The **BLACK BEAR** is not accurately named, since its fur is not always this colour. This omnivore is found primarily in Yosemite National Park, weighing as much as 160 kilograms (352 pounds) when fully grown.

BOB CAT or bay lynx. This animal is well camouflaged by its yellowish-brown spotted coat; it hunts at night and, in dry regions, obtains the water it needs to survive from its prey.

The **CACTUS WREN,** a species of wren nesting primarily in the cholla cactus, it feeds on the insects and spiders living in the yucca palm.

COYOTES. As omnivores, coyotes are well suited for survival in the desert. They eat insects, grass, tortoises and fruit, but primarily rely on carrion.

CYPRINODONS, Death Valley National Monument. In the warmer seasons, small freshwater fish known as cyprinodons can be seen swimming in a stream near Salt Creek. This rare breed that initially lived 20,000 years ago in the ice age lakes has adapted to a salt water environment.

GAMBEL'S QUAIL. This bird breeds mainly during the rainy seasons. In dry periods it can lose so much water that its body weight is halved.

The **GOLDEN EAGLE** lives primarily in the northern hemisphere. In southern California it nests in crevices in the rocks in the vicinity of yucca palms. It lives on rabbits and large rodents.

GOPHER SNAKE. This species of snake hunts the rodents that are its prey by digging up the ground with its head; it is only active in the evening.

GRAY FOX: an aggressive species of fox that hunts those lizards, rodents and birds found in trees.

HORNED LIZARD. This cold-blooded animal regulates its body temperature by contracting in hot sun so that a smaller surface area is exposed to the heat. In cooler weather it spreads itself out on the ground in order to absorb as much sun as possible.

JACK RABBIT. A nocturnal animal living in hollows and the shadow of bushes, the jack rabbit regulates its body temperature by means of its unusually large ears.

KANGAROO RAT. This rodent lives in burrows underground where the temperature is more constant than on the surface. It also stores seeds underground so that they absorb moisture and in this way, obtains all the water it needs.

KIT FOX. A fox with thick skin on its paws, it has strikingly large ears which conduct the heat away from its body preventing it from becoming too hot. A thick growth of hair between the toes helps it move over sand.

The **MOUNTAIN QUAIL** is a bird which lives in the higher regions of the desert, feeding on insects and green acorns.

MOURNING DOVE. When temperatures are low this dove can survive for several days without water, but when temperatures are very high it needs a great deal of liquid: the water evaporates through its beak and respiratory organs, thus keeping this small bird cool.

Lighthouse at Big Sur.

MULE DEER. This animal mainly inhabits regions above 1,000 metres (3,250 feet); it can survive short-term shortages of water without serious consequences.

PHAINOPOPLA, a black bird otherwise known as the silky flycatcher. It obtains sufficient liquids from its food, insects in the spring and summer, mistletoe berries in the winter, to survive without drinking water.

The **POOR-WILL** is the only bird of prey hibernating in winter. The colouring of its plumage blends in with its surroundings.

The **RATTLESNAKE** spends the daylight hours in burrows or under stones to protect it from the sun. A small heat-sensitive pit between the eyes and nostrils enables it to detect its warm-blooded prey. In cold weather this poisonous reptile creeps into deep crevices in the rocks.

RED-SPOTTED TOAD. Well-adapted to its barren desert surroundings, this toad absorbs water from the soil when it sits on the ground, through a thin place on its skin on the underside of its body.

ROSYBOA. This very rare species of snake lives mainly in rocky environments, where it is protected from natural enemies and from the heat. It is an expert climber.

SCRUB JAY. A bird which lives in the higher regions of the desert where pines and small oaks grow, it lives on seeds or when these are not available, on insects.

The **SHOVEL-NOSED SNAKE** is only to be found in the desert. It burrows in the sand with its ideally-shaped, shovel-like head to protect itself from the sun and from its enemies.

SIDE-BLOTCHED LIZARD. This type of lizard is well-adapted to living in the most barren of desert regions. It blends in so well with the ground it is very difficult to spot.

SIDEWINDER. A snake which moves forward at high speeds across the sand by a sideways looping motion, it is protected by its camouflaging colour. It also burrows into the ground to escape the heat.

The **STINKBUG** drives away its predators by means of a repellent smell. When in danger it freezes in an upright position and this alone frightens most attackers away. It is a scavenger that feeds on decaying matter and dead plants.

TARANTULA. This poisonous wolf spider is protected from the sun by thick hair. It eats beetles and grasshoppers and its powerful bite causes a painful inflammation.

TERMITES live in the flesh of the yucca palm fruit, which prevents them from drying up in the heat; they feed on the dead wood of the bark.

TORTOISE. This animal is able to convert its food into moisture and carries approximately half a litre (one pint) of water in two pouches under its shell. It protects itself from the heat of the sun by crawling into holes in the ground and hibernates both in the hot summer months and in winter when food is in short supply; its camouflaging colour protects it from its natural enemies.

The **TREE FROG** blends in with its surroundings, and in this way is protected from its natural enemies. It lives in small pools of water in the rocks, and its body temperature is regulated through the evaporation of body fluids.

WHIP TAIL LIZARD. This lizard is mainly to be found near water, burrowing into the ground; like the badger, it uses its front legs to dig for its prey.

The **WOODPECKER**, found in Joshua Tree National Monument, usually nests in the trunk of the Joshua tree, although other palms and cacti are also sometimes chosen. It feeds on the insects that inhabit the yucca palm.

The **WOOD RAT** lives near the yucca palm which provides it with a cool and shady environment.

YUCCA MOTH. This moth lays its eggs in the flowers of the yucca palm, the fruit providing nutrition for its larvae.

The **YUCCA NIGHT LIZARD** is one of the smallest species of lizard in the United States. It is thickly scaled and lives in dead yucca palm branches or trunks.

MINERALS

BORAX, a crystal consisting primarily of water, sodium and boron. It can be melted down to make borax glass as well as being used in industry and for medicinal purposes.

PINTO GNEISS, Joshua Tree National Monument, a metamorphic black stone formed around 800 million years ago

Sand dunes in Death Valley.

through the heating up and compression of gravel and sand beneath the deposits of the lake in Pinto Basin.

NATIONAL PARKS AND OTHER SIGHTS

The numbers in italics refer to colour photographs.

INFORMATION is provided by the U.S. Park Service, an institution of the Department of the Interior responsible for national parks. The Park Rangers, recognized by their broad-brimmed hats, will answer most questions. Up-to-date information about the park, free maps and programmes of events are obtainable from the Visitors' Centres. There are also exhibitions, slide shows, films and lectures about the geology, vegetation, animals and history of the region. For hikes lasting more than one day, a backcountry permit, issued free of charge, is required.

AGUA CALIENTE INDIAN RESERVATION. Half of this reservation is located in the Palm Springs region.

ANCIENT BRISTLECONE PINE FOREST. An area of ancient pines situated in the White Mountains. *30, 31*

BIG SUR, a coastal area on the edge of the Santa Lucia Range south of Monterey on State Highway 1, characterized by steep, rugged cliffs. After the Second World War, people came here in search of a simpler life away from modern civilization; one famous resident was Henry Miller. Later on, Big Sur was also discovered by the upper classes of San Francisco.

CALICO GHOST TOWN. This town had its heyday during the silver rush of 1881 to 1896. From 1881 to 1907, the Calico Mining District was a source of silver and borates. Silver mining continued here until 1946. Today Calico Ghost Town is a museum.

DEATH VALLEY NATIONAL MONUMENT, established in 1933 and open all year round; the best time to visit is from October to April. With a total area of approximately 809,000 hectares (1,990,000 acres), the area consists of a basin with no outlet measuring some 220 kilometres (130 miles) long and 25 kilometres (15 miles) wide. It is located partly in eastern California and partly in Nevada. The climate is hot and dry, with maximum temperatures reaching 57 degrees Centigrade (134 degrees Fahrenheit). Outstanding features include the Stove Pipe Wells sand dunes (42 square kilometres/16.2 square miles), the jagged salt formations of Devil's Golf Course, and the enormous salt flats covering an area of 500 square kilometres (193 square miles). Badwater is one of the lowest points in the western hemisphere. The main viewpoints are Dante's View (1,669 metres/5,475 feet) looking out over the whole of Death Valley and Badwater, and Zabriskie Point with a view across the treeless landscape of the desert. Furnace Creek hosts the Borax Museum, Death Valley Visitors' Centre, date palms and, nearby, the remains of the Harmony Borax Works. In the northern part of the valley are Ubehebe Crater (around 152 metres or 494 feet deep) and Scotty's Castle dating from the 1920s. Comprising the region's wildlife are the desert bighorn sheep, rabbit, antelope ground squirrel, as well as various insects, snakes, birds, lizards, toads, wild cats and even fish. The survival of the animals is facilitated by the existence of over 600 different types of plant. Although there is very little precipitation and most of it evaporates, some moisture does seep into the earth. It can then be absorbed by the widely branching roots of the plants which have adapted to the conditions of the desert. *37, 38/39, 41, 42/43*

Aguereberry Point, located near Emigrant Canyon. An ideal viewpoint for taking photographs (approximately 1,960 metres or 6,370 feet high) looking out over Death Valley and the Funeral Mountains to the east.

Artist's Drive, south of the Furnace Creek Area, is eight kilometres (five miles) of panoramic road through mineral-coloured mountains. The pink, red and yellow colouring is due to the presence of iron salts, the green to decomposing mica and the reddish-purple to manganese.

Ashford Mill Ruins. In 1914, gold was extracted at this mill from the ores brought out of the Golden Treasure Mine eight kilometres (five miles) away. The mine is said to have been originally sold for 50,000 dollars to a Hungarian aristocrat, who later re-sold it for 105,000 dollars.

Badwater, located south of the Furnace Creek. One of the lowest points in the western hemisphere, it is 85 metres (278 feet) below sea level. Nearby are two survey points 86 metres (282 feet) below sea level.

Borax Museum, Furnace Creek Ranch, an open-air exhibition with displays of mining processes and equipment.

Charcoal Kilns, near Wildrose Canyon. From 1870 on, charcoal was produced here for a series of melting furnaces.

Dante's View, some 21 kilometres (12.6 miles) from the Furnace Creek-Death Valley Junction Highway: a splendid view of Death Valley from a height of approximately 1,669 metres (5,424 feet).

Death Valley, in geological terms a very recent valley, formed around 10 million years ago as a result of movement in the earth' interior, through the displacement and fracturing of the earth. Later the fractured rock joined up again to form what is known as breccia, rock consisting of angular fragments. This slow geological process continues today.

Devil's Cornfield, east of Stove Pipe Wells, features salt crystals exposed by erosion as well as isolated clusters of bushes.

Devil's Golf Course, a large field south of Furnace Creek covered with salt formations.

Furnace Creek Ranch, a central tourist area open throughout the year, with a Visitor Centre, accommodation and golf course.

Harmony Borax Works Ruins, north of the Furnace Creek Area. Borax was produced here during the 1880s; the original buildings have been restored.

Mosaic Canyon, near Store Pipe wells, a canyon with colourful walls.

Natural Bridge, south of the Furnace Creek Area: a natural arch formed when the canyon was flooded.

Rhyolite Ghost Town, east of Beatty: famous in particular for its Bottle House, built with 50,000 bottles.

Salt Creek, between Stove Pipe Wells and Furnace Creek: habitat of the small pupfish.

Sand Dunes, east of Stove Pipe Wells: an area that also stays warm during the winter, with sand dunes.

Scotty's Castle. Its owner called the building a castle, with some twenty-five rooms, more than a dozen chimneys and even a real waterfall.

Stove Pipe Wells, a tourist centre with accommodation.

Telescope Peak, south of Wildrose Canyon: the highest point of the national monument, 3,368 metres (11,049 feet) above sea level.

Titus Canyon, near Rhyolite: a canyon with rocks of many different colours.

Ubehebe Crater, near Scotty's Castle: an impressive crater 152 metres (494 feet) deep, formed by a massive volcanic eruption.

Zabriskie Point, a famous viewpoint looking out over the weathered hills formed by erosion and a treeless desert. It was named for Christian Brevoort Zabriskie (1864 – 1936), General Director of the Pacific Coast Borax Company for thirty-five years.

JOSHUA TREE NATIONAL MONUMENT.

Established in 1936, this National Monument is located in the central part of Southern California, around 232 kilometres (145 miles) east of Los Angeles; it is approximately 223,000 hectares (551,033 acres) in area and open all year round. Spring is the best time to visit, when the desert flowers are in bloom. It is here that the sea of rocks meets the barren wastes of the Mojave and Colorado Deserts. At midday the ground temperatures can rise to over 82 degrees Centigrade (174 degrees Fahrenheit), when most of the water evaporates before seeping into the ground. The Joshua trees and cacti are to be found in the higher, wetter areas of the Mojave Desert, while the creosote bush, ironwood and ocotillo grow in the Colorado Desert. The national monument is home to a variety of insects, the bighorn sheep, coyote, squirrel and numerous species of birds, including the eagle. Many of the animals have adapted to the desert conditions: in the daytime they burrow deep into the sand while they also suck water out of plants and the body fluids of their prey. It is important to be on one's guard against poisonous spiders, scorpions and rattlesnakes. The plants, most being rather stunted, are adapted to the hot, dry climate: they shed their leaves and store water. *2, 44*

Cholla Cactus Garden, an interesting garden featuring the species of cactus known as the bigelow cholla. Also growing here are the creosote bush, teddybear cholla, holycross cholla and desert senna.

Cottonwood Spring, an important source of water at the time of the gold rush. At the beginning of the century, around 11,000 litres (2,420 gallons) of water were pumped out of this spring every day, in order to supply the Iron Chief Mine 30 kilometres (18 miles) away in the Eagle Mountains. Later the amount of water yielded by the spring dropped to a few litres a day, but in 1971, an earthquake displaced the water table to such an extent that now almost 2,500 litres (548 gallons) can be pumped up daily. Palms and a type of willow known as cottonwood were planted by gold prospectors around the turn of the century. The palm oasis is well-known for its numerous species of birdlife.

Hidden Valley, a protected valley completely enclosed by cliffs. Access is only via a narrow path leading past scattered rocks. The valley is rumoured to have been the favourite hideaway of cattle thieves, since it is almost hermetically sealed.

Indian Cove. An area with interesting rock formations and caves inhabited by bighorn sheep. The boulders contain feldspar crystals.

Indian Mounds. The Serrano, Cahuilla and Chemehuevi Indians lived in this area, hunting the bighorn sheep, antelope and rabbit as well as gathering fruit and nuts. Evidence of their culture remains in drawings on the rocks, and various bones and stones shaped into different forms.

Keys View. A summit in the Little San Bernardino Mountains with a splendid view of the Salton Sea, San Andreas Fault, Mount San Jacinto, Mount San Gorgonio and the desert landscape stretching as far as the Mexican border.

Pinto Basin, once a fertile region with adequate vegetation and a lake formed around 6,000 years ago after the last ice age. In prehistoric times the basin was inhabited by the Indians, who were forced to leave the area when it dried out. Later on it was settled by nomadic tribes.

KLAMATH MOUNTAINS, a very rugged mountainous region in northern California and Oregon approximately 31,000 square kilometres (18,000 square miles) in area. The Klamath Mountains are made up of a number of small ranges: the Siskiyou, Trinity, Trinity Alps, Marble, Scott Bar, South Fork and Salmon Mountains. Most of the peaks are in the 1,500 to 2,100 metre range (4,875 to 6,825 feet) while only Mount Hilton, (2,732 metres or 8,879 feet) is appreciably higher.

LAKE TAHOE: a 35 kilometre (21 mile) long lake situated 1,899 metres (5,697 feet) above sea level on the border with Nevada. The lake and the nearby mountains are a popular holiday and winter sports area. *24/25*

LASSEN VOLCANIC NATIONAL PARK. Situated in the northern part of California in the Cascade Range, this park is 430 square kilometres (166 square miles) in area. It was granted national monument status in 1907 and became a national park in 1916. The last time Lassen Peak (3,187 metres or 10,355 feet) erupted was in 1914, after 400 years of inactivity; further eruptions

are still thought possible. The volcano is named after the Dane Peter Lassen, who conducted treks at the time of the gold rush and used the volcano as a landmark. A 48 kilometre (30 mile) long road running through the park provides access to numerous sights: lakes, fields of lava blocks, solidified lava flows, hot springs and bubbling mud. *16/17, 19, 20, 21, 23*

Mount Shasta, a 4,317 metre (14,030 foot) peak in the Cascade Range which is permanently covered in snow and ice.

LAVA BEDS NATIONAL MONU-MENT, an 18,600 hectare (45,960 acre) moon-like volcanic area in Northern California on the Oregon

Lassen Volcanic National Park.

border, with Tule Lake to the north. Hiking trails lead to numerous lava and ice caves, lava flows, fumaroles and pillars.

REDWOOD NATIONAL PARK is located in the farthest northwestern corner of California on the Pacific Ocean. It stretches for approximately 64 kilometres (40 miles) and covers an area of some 40,000 hectares (10,964 acres). The park was established in 1968 and is open all year round. The highest tree in the world, known as The Tall Tree, is situated near Redwood Creek near the town of Orick, at the southern

end of the park. Redwood National Park has deer, elk, the antelope ground squirrel, beaver, and woodpeckers in addition to wild cats and bears.

Redwood Creek, a grove with three of the six tallest trees in the world including the highest, a 112 metre (364 foot) redwood known as The Tall Tree.

The Tall Tree, a coast redwood discovered in 1963 in Redwood National Park.

SEQUOIA NATIONAL PARK and **KING'S CANYON NATIONAL PARK.** Located in eastern California, both parks are open all year long though there may be periods in the winter when snow makes them inaccessible. The best time to visit is from June to September. Sequoia National Park has an area of approximately 160,000 hectares (395,360 acres), King's Canyon National Park around 184,000 hectares (454,670 acres). They are administered jointly, forming a tract of unspoilt countryside stretching from north to south with mountains, canyons and giant sequoias. Sequoia National Park, the southern part, is in the Sierra Mountains; at the eastern edge of the park is Mount Whitney and General Sherman Tree stands in the Giant Forest. In the westernmost part of King's Canyon National Park are the giant trees General Grant and General Lee, located in Grant Grove. From here a 48 kilometre (30 mile) highway follows the winding course of the King's River through King's River Canyon, which is 2,438 metres (7,923 feet) deep, and Cedar Grove. Among the animals to be found in this park are wild cats, the silver fox, puma, antelope ground squirrel, coyote, black bear, porcupine, mule deer, woodpecker, rattlesnake and skunk. *33*

Auto Log. A tree trunk with a circumference measuring over six metres (19 feet), which fell in 1917.

Buttress Tree. This 2,300 year old sequoia tree, which fell in 1959, has a length of 83 metres (270 feet) and a maximum circumference of seven metres (22 feet). Sequoias fall when

The golden age is over: Bodie Ghost Town.

their roots, which are spread flat under the surface of the earth, lose their hold.

General Grant Tree, the second largest tree in the world (measured by height and circumference) with a height of 81.5 metres (264.5 feet) and a circumference of 32.8 metres (106.4 feet). It was discovered in 1862 and is approximately 2,000 years old. The tree is named after Ulysses Simpson Grant, the eighteenth president of the United States (1869–1877).

General Sherman Tree, the largest tree in the world measured by height

and circumference. It is around 2,500 years old, has a height of approximately 83.8 metres (274.4 feet) and a circumference of 31.3 metres (100.9 feet). General Sherman was the commander-in-chief of the Union Army in the American Civil War.

Giant Forest, a grove where giant trees such as the General Sherman, General Lee and Chief Sequoia are located.

Moro Rock, a rounded granite rock 2,050 metres (6,662 feet) above sea level, with a relative height of 1,219 metres (3,978 feet) above the valley. The rock's shape is the result of exfoliation. From its top, there is a magnificent view of the Middle Fork Kaweah River and Lake Kaweah. *33*

Mount Stewart, named after the publisher George W. Stewart of Visalia, one of the founders of Sequoia National Park.

Mount Whitney, 4,417 metres (14,495 feet) above sea level, the highest mountain in California.

Redwood Mountain Grove, the largest stand of giant sequoias.

Tunnel Log, a giant tree which toppled in 1937. With a length of approximately 84 metres (273 feet) and a maximum circumference of six metres (19 feet), it forms a tunnel 2.4 metres (14.4 feet) high and 5 metres (16 feet) wide.

Tunnel Rock, a tunnel built in 1934 through a granite cliff, to replace the road that originally circumvented it.

SQUAW VALLEY, northwest of Lake Tahoe, a well-known winter sports area with a wide variety of facilities.

TWENTY-NINE PALMS DESERT HOUSE. This desert oasis, with wells and houses made of mud and brick, served as a cattle-breeding site and at the beginning of the nineteenth century, as an overnight stop for waggoners en route to the gold mines.

YOSEMITE NATIONAL PARK, established in 1890 and open all year round, though it may be inaccessible at certain times in the winter. It is located in the Sierra Mountains in the eastern part of California, 305 kilometres (183 miles) east of San Francisco or 515 kilometres (309 miles) north of Los Angeles. It measures 80 by 64 kilometres (50 by 40 miles) with a total area of 3,000 square kilometres (1,189 square miles). Characteristic features of the park are mountains, meadows, forests and rivers with the high waterfalls Yosemite and Bridalveil. Its mountains include El Capitan (2,307 metres/7,569 feet) and Half Dome (2,694 metres/8,842 feet). Glacier Point (2,198 metres/7,214 feet) above Yosemite Valley commands a view of the Sierra Nevadas. The Tuolumne Meadows are also worth visiting. Near the south entrance, on the road to Fresno, is Mariposa Grove housing giant trees with circumferences of up to 29 metres (94 feet) and heights of up to 71 metres (230 feet). There are many different kinds of animals here, in particular bears, deer and rodents. *6/7, 9,11, 12, 13, 15, 27*

Bodie Ghost Town, located east of Yosemite National Park on the Nevada border, dating from the time of the gold rush. On display are mine buildings and mining equipment.

Bridalveil Falls, Yosemite Valley, 189 metres (614 feet) high. There is a good viewpoint nearby.

El Capitan, a steep granite cliff on the north side of the Merced River in Yosemite Valley, 914 metres (2,970 feet)

Seventeen-Mile Drive near Monterey.

above the valley and 2,307 metres (7,569 feet) above sea level.

Glacier Point, a magnificent viewpoint looking out over Yosemite Valley, 2,198 metres (7,214 feet) above sea level, and 915 metres (2,974 feet) above the valley.

Half Dome. The northwestern half of this massif, scored with fissures, suffered erosion by the Tenaya Glacier, while the southeastern half remained intact. The rounded form is the result of exfoliation.

Indian Village, a restored Awanichi village with an exhibition. Around 1860 most of the Awanichi Indians were forced to leave this area, and only those employed today in the national park still live in Yosemite Valley.

Mariposa Grove, located at the southern end of the park and famous for its numerous giant trees.

Mono Lake. A 200 square kilometre (772 square mile) salt lake east of Yosemite National Park fed by streams from the Sierra Mountains. It is famous for its tufa formations, up to 14 metres (45 feet) in height. This body of water, which has no outlet, is slowly drying out since many of the streams flowing into it have been diverted. The increasing concentration of salt is endangering the habitat of the migrating water fowl. *34/35*

Tioga Road, a scenic route crossing the national park from east to west leading over the highest pass in the Sierra Nevadas, the Tioga Pass (3,350 metres or 10,887 feet above sea level).

Tuolumne Meadows, subalpine meadows 2,620 metres (8,600 feet) above sea level.

Yosemite Falls, Yosemite Valley, on the northern bank of the Merced River: total height 739 metres (2,425 feet); consists of the 436 metre (1,430 feet) Upper Fall and the 97 metre (315 feet) Lower Fall, in addition to several smaller cascades.

Yosemite Valley. The centre of the national park with spectacular granite walls and giant waterfalls. There are numerous tourist facilities in this U-shaped valley, some 11 kilometres (6.6 miles) long and 1 kilometre wide. The valley was once covered by a glacier-fed lake; today the Merced River flows through it from east to west. Yosemite Valley is particularly famous for its waterfalls, namely Bridalveil Falls and Yosemite Falls.

LIST OF SOURCES AND ILLUSTRATIONS

Edward Abbey, *The Journey Home.* New York: E. P. Dutton, 1977. Copyright © 1977 by Edward Abbey. Used by permission of the publisher, Dutton, an imprint of New American Library, a division of Penguin Books USA Inc.
Alonzo Delano, *Life on the Plains and Among the Diggings.* New York: 1854.
Jack Kerouac, *On the Road.* London: 1958.
John Muir, *My First Summer in the Sierra.* Boston: Houghton Mifflin Company, 1911. *Our National Parks.* Boston: Houghton Mifflin Company, 1901. *The Mountains of California.* New York: Century Company, 1911. *The Yosemite.* New York: Double-day & Company, Inc., 1962.
John Steinbeck, *Travels with Charley.* New York: The Viking Press, 1961.
Walt Whitman, "Leaves of Grass", in *Complete Poetry and Collected Prose.* New York: The Viking Press, 1982.

We thank all copyright holders for their permission to reprint. Those we were not able to reach are asked to contact us.

The map on page 48 was drawn by Christine Hartl.

DESTINATION CALIFORNIA
NATIONAL PARKS
WINDSOR BOOKS INTERNATIONAL, 1992

© 1987 by Verlag C. J. Bucher GmbH
Revised in 1992
Munich and Berlin
Translation: Sue Bollans
Editor: Karen Lemiski
Anthology: Carmel Finnan
All rights reserved
Printed and bound in Germany
ISBN 1 874111 05 7